Women Today

Minorities

by
Gisela Meier

The Rourke Corporation, Inc.
Vero Beach, Florida 32964

Copyright 1991 by The Rourke Corporation, Inc.

All rights reserved. No part of this book may be reproduced or utilized in any form or by any means, electronic or mechanical, including photocopying, recording or by any information storage and retrieval system without permission in writing from the publisher.

The Rourke Corporation, Inc.
P.O. Box 3328, Vero Beach, FL 32964

Meier, Gisela.
   Minorities / by Gisela Meier.
     p. cm. —(Women today)
   Includes bibliographical references and index.
   Summary: Describes the image, culture, family life, working conditions, and future of Black, Hispanic, and Asian-American women living in the United States.
   ISBN 0-86593-124-0
   1. Minority women—United States—Juvenile literature. [1. Minority women.] I. Title. II. Series.
HQ1410.M44 1991
305.48'9693—dc20   91-11651
                                                                 CIP
                                                                   AC

Series Editor: Elizabeth Sirimarco
Editors: Gregory Lee, Marguerite Aronowitz
Book design and production: The Creative Spark, Capistrano Beach, California
Cover Photograph: Elizabeth Crews/The Image Works

Contents

1. Images Of Minority Women — 4
2. Black Women — 10
3. Hispanic Women — 22
4. Asian-American Women — 36
5. A Look At The '80s — 46
6. Into The Future — 54

   Glossary — 60

   Bibliography — 62

   Index — 64

1 Images Of Minority Women

On television, American society often looks completely integrated. Everyone can be whatever they want to be, no matter what their skin color, whether they are male or female.

It wasn't always like that. In the 1950s and early '60s, people who watched TV saw only white men in important and powerful positions. Women on TV were mostly white and usually portrayed as housewives and mothers. Women of color, when they did appear on television, generally were servants or menial workers.

Today, television shows us women of all colors in many different roles, both on news programs and in fictional shows. We see black, Hispanic and Asian women who are newscasters, elected officials, judges, lawyers, doctors, police officers, and business leaders.

In fields that were once reserved for men or whites, minority women are making a name for themselves. Among them are black tennis star Zina Garrison, Olympic ice skaters Debbie Thomas and Tiffany Chin, and Olympic track stars Florence Griffith-Joyner and Jackie Joyner-Kersee. One of the most popular television journalists is Connie Chung. Recent best-seller lists have included books by black writers Alice Walker and Toni Morrison, and Chinese-American authors Amy Tan and Maxine Hong Kingston.

Barbara Harris, the first female bishop in the history of the Episcopal Church, is black. The first female investment banker at Merrill Lynch, Josie Natori, is from the Philippines.

During the past decade Hispanic women have held important posts in the federal government, including Katherine Ortega, who served as U.S. Treasurer, and Linda Chavez, former staff director of the federal Civil Rights Commission. In 1989, Ileana Ros-Lehtinen became the first Hispanic woman elected to Congress.

A 1989 Gallup poll asked Americans what 10 women they most admired. Number six on the list was Oprah Winfrey, an actress and talk show host, and the first black woman to own a television and movie-production studio.

It's easy to think that the problems of the past have been solved. Has America really become a just society where anyone, regardless of skin color or sex, has equal opportunities?

To some extent, the answer is yes. The *civil rights movement* and the *feminist movement* of the 1960s knocked down many of the barriers that kept racial minorities and women out of certain schools, sports, jobs, and other areas that were off limits.

Since then, millions of minority women have graduated from colleges and universities. They have found important and satisfying jobs. Many have started successful businesses.

But this is only part of the picture.

American women as a group still earn less than American men. For every dollar a man earns, a woman earns only 66 cents. The average black woman earns less than the average white woman, and the average Hispanic woman earns less than either of them.

Asian-American women are the exception. On the average, their earnings nearly equal or even surpass those of white women. However, Asian women who are recent immigrants—such as the Vietnamese—tend to earn much lower wages.

One reason women earn less than men is that most of them work in what are known as "pink collar" occupations: teaching, nursing, and secretarial or other office jobs. Occupations traditionally held by women (for example, nursing) pay less than those usually held by men (such as truck drivers). Women of color are even more likely to have low-paying jobs.

The White-Collar World

More women have been moving up the executive ranks during the past 20 years. In 1988, nearly 40 percent of management positions were held by women,

The women's liberation movement shared much in common with the civil rights movement: Both represented a large group of people who had been denied the rights enjoyed by the white American male.

compared to 26 percent in 1978. But only three percent of these women managers were minorities.

Women of all colors are finding that their climb up the business ladder comes to a stop before they can get to top-level positions. Most of those jobs are still filled by white males. Among the top executives of the largest companies in America, less than two percent are women. And a fraction of these are women of color.

Even when women get big promotions, they don't earn as much as men. Women who work as managers, for example, even in top corporate positions, are paid about 40 percent less than men in similar positions.

At the bottom of the economic scale, the past years have seen the *feminization of poverty*. Of all American adults below the *poverty line* (defined as a family income less than $12,000 per year), more than 60 percent are women—most of them single mothers.

As members of minority groups, women of color are even more likely to fall below the poverty line. In 1988, 10 percent of the white population was impoverished, but almost 32 percent of blacks and nearly 27 percent of Hispanics fell below the poverty line. Poverty rates for some of the immigrant Asian groups go as high as 20 percent.

Of the more than nine million blacks living in poverty in 1988, three out of four lived in families headed by women. Nearly half of the five million poor Hispanics lived in households maintained by single women.

Unemployment is higher among black and Hispanic women than it is among white women. According to 1989 figures from the U.S. Department of Labor, eight percent of Hispanic women and ten percent of black women were unemployed, as compared to four percent of white women.

Challenges

During the past decades, more and more women of all colors have been taking jobs. Today 68 percent of women who have children under age 18 are employed. All of them share common problems. They worry about finding the right job to suit their talents and financial needs. Balancing the demands of being a parent and having a job is another concern. Just two problems that working mothers encounter are keeping up with the housekeeping, and finding day-care for their children.

Although there have been dramatic advances in the workplace, there are still battles to be won: access to top-level positions and salaries, better pay for pink collar jobs, and better day-care arrangements for women with children.

Along with those concerns, minority women have their own particular problems. One of these is *racism*.

In spite of the progress made during the past 30 years, racism is still a powerful obstacle. Proof can be seen in statistics, in their lower earnings, and in the lack of women of color in high-level positions. It can also be seen in the news. There are still incidents of racially-motivated vandalism and violence. The Ku Klux Klan and similar white power groups are still active.

Many women of color still encounter racism in their neighborhoods, their schools, and their workplaces. Sometimes it is subtle. People treat them differently or have certain expectations about them because of their color. Other times it is blatant and vicious. Strangers attack them with insults and threats.

In addition, the millions of women who came to America from Asia and Latin America during the past two decades have their own challenges. Many of them must deal with the trauma of being separated from their homelands and families. They must learn a new language and adjust to the culture and lifestyles of their new environment. Many find themselves in an emotional tug-of-war, caught between the traditions and values of their native land and the demands of their new country.

2 Black Women

She's a woman anyone would admire. Elegant, witty and self-assured, she is a practicing attorney as well as a wise and loving mother.

She is happily married to a doctor and lives in a lovely, upscale home. Claire Huxtable, a fictional character on television's *The Cosby Show*, is the image of the successful black woman.

But television sometimes shows us another image of the American black woman. She's a teenager living in a shabby ghetto apartment. She didn't finish high school because she got pregnant and dropped out. She has no job, no skills and no husband, so she supports herself and her two small children by collecting welfare payments.

Both the successful attorney and the poor unwed mother are accurate portrayals of some black women in America today. But neither image tells the whole story.

The story of black women in America today is one of great advances and desperate problems. Millions of black women and their families live in middle- and upper-class neighborhoods and work in well-paying jobs. Millions of others live in hopeless poverty in the crumbling, crime-ridden inner cities.

Good News And Bad

For many black women, life today is better than it was 30 years ago. Both the civil rights movement and the feminist movement helped black women start on a dramatic march toward equality.

Black women are no longer barred from schools, colleges, and jobs. Laws that kept black women from voting and running for office have been eliminated.

Almost 80 percent of black women now get high school diplomas, and about one-third go on to college. In terms of the kinds of jobs they get and the money they earn, black women are nearly equal to white women.

Today, black women are lawyers, judges, doctors,

Breaking the high-tech job barriers: This woman is a product development specialist at a Texas computer software firm.

journalists, corporate managers, business owners, and college presidents. In 1989, there were 1,814 black women holding public office—more than three times as many as in 1975.

Overall, black women have done much better during the past two decades than black men. While black working women earn nearly as much as white women, black men earn on average much less than white men. The unemployment rate for black men is higher than that for white women, and more than double than for white men. More black women than black men complete high school, graduate from college, and earn post-graduate degrees.

There are a number of reasons why black women have done so much better than black men. First, most of the new jobs created during the past two decades have been in areas such as management, bookkeeping, sales, and secretarial work. These jobs traditionally have been held mainly by women. Second, black men seem to bear the brunt of racism, because black women are seen as less threatening.

Affirmative action programs that encourage the hiring of women and minorities often give black women an advantage. By employing a black woman a company improves its status in two areas at once.

But there is bad news, too. Women of all colors continue to earn only 66 cents for every dollar earned by a white man. Earnings for black women are somewhat lower at 62 cents for every dollar.

During the 1980s the proportion of blacks below the poverty line increased, while the proportion of blacks earning middle-class wages began to drop. This was true even for blacks who had earned college degrees. The portion of college-educated blacks earning middle-class salaries dropped from more than 17 percent in 1979 to about 13 percent in 1987.

According to one study, 407,000 black women finished at least four years of college between 1979 and 1987. Yet the number of college-educated black women who earned middle-class wages dropped during those years by 10,000.

There also has been an increase in the number of black women who are raising children alone. The number of black families headed by women jumped from 1.3 million in 1970 to 3 million in 1987. More than seven out of ten of those families live in poverty.

Changes in the economy during the last decade have had an effect on Americans of all colors. Many economists say that the gap between the upper class and the lowest class became wider. In other words, the rich got richer and the poor got poorer.

Today, there are nearly twice as many whites as blacks who are below the poverty line. But a greater proportion of blacks live in poverty. In 1988, nearly one

13

Bishop Barbara Harris faced both racism and sexism when she became the first woman ever ordained by the Episcopal Church.

in every three blacks was below the poverty line. Among whites, one in ten was impoverished.

Ironically, the success of many black people may be contributing to the despair of blacks in the inner city. Thirty years ago, the ghettos were home to both poor and successful blacks because racial discrimination kept most black families from moving into middle-class neighborhoods. More affluent black families helped support businesses in the ghettos and provided models that children could imitate.

These communities started breaking up in the 1960s, when middle-class blacks were able to move to other areas. As a result, the ghettos lost both the business and the role models those families had provided. At the same time, many companies transferred their headquarters from the cities to the suburbs and manufacturers closed their urban plants. Left with no jobs, the ghettos became more isolated than ever.

The Vanishing Black Man

Many young black women of all economic classes have no black men with whom to share their lives. Their prospects of finding someone to marry and raise a family with are slim.

"We are losing them," laments a writer in a recent issue of *Ebony* magazine. "Not just in small, isolated numbers but by the scores. Every day, every hour, more and more slip away until they are beyond reach and hope. They are young black men in trouble—young black men in crisis. They are our sons, our brothers, our lovers—our future."

"I'm 27 years old and I'm dateless," says a black woman who works as an assistant to a congressman. "What's so incredible is—because of my job—I'm constantly out there meeting people, but it's a rare day that I see a young, black, serious-minded man."

Why is there a shortage of black men?

Numerous black men have seen their jobs disappear

during the past 20 years. Many industrial companies—such as steel production and automobile manufacturing—have either closed down or moved their plants out of the country. Unfortunately, few black men have the training or education needed to qualify for new high-tech, white-collar jobs opening up in the 1990s.

Unemployment is a major problem for black men. Nearly 23 percent between the ages of 16 and 24 are unemployed, more than twice the rate for young white men. Unable to support their families, they often end up leaving so their wives and children can receive welfare assistance. A household headed by an unemployed male receives much lower payments.

Frustrated and desperate, many young blacks turn to drug dealing and other crime as a way of making money and achieving status. They often become victims of violence, and many are arrested. One of every four black men in their 20s is in jail, in prison, on probation, or on parole.

Homicide is the number one cause of death for black men between the ages of 15 and 25. They are ten times more likely to be murdered than white men in the same age bracket. (Homicide is also the leading cause of death for black women ages 15 to 34.)

"If we cannot turn these numbers around, they threaten the very existence of the race," said Beverly Cole, director of education and health for the National Association for the Advancement of Colored People (NAACP).

The Inner City Woman

Along with the tragic crisis of the black man, there is a great deal of concern about black women in the inner city. Unmarried teenagers continue to have children. Is this adding to the problems of poverty?

Most blacks say no. In fact, the number of babies born to black teenagers has actually decreased since the 1970s. The real problem is that the number of marriages

Black women as a group make up a large share of single-parent households in the United States.

has been dropping because there are not enough marriageable black men. According to this theory, more teenage mothers are victims of poverty, not a cause of it.

Either way, young single mothers are part of a cycle of poverty that will repeat itself with the next generation. For example, many black female teenagers drop out of high school, so they have no job skills. They also know little about raising children. They don't know how to motivate their youngsters or help them get the skills they need to break out of poverty.

These children then grow up without a father, with a mother who doesn't work, and with few signs of hope or chances to better themselves. More often than not, they grow up to be unemployed fathers and single

Toni Morrison is one of America's most critically acclaimed novelists, male or female, black or white.

mothers, still trapped in the ghetto and making the overall problem worse.

"Almost a generation has passed since these events began to unfold, but we now have a second generation of African-Americans who have come to accept poverty and dependency as a way of life," says Joyce A. Ladner, a professor of sociology at Howard University.

Tragically, many inner city women turn to drugs. Some become prostitutes to raise money to buy *crack*. Every year, crack-addicted women give birth to about 100,000 addicted babies. Because they are unable to care for their children, the job of raising them is often passed on to the grandmothers or other family members.

Racism

Unlike other minorities in America, the first blacks to arrive here did not come by choice. They were forced to come as slaves. When a black woman looks back over the history of her people in America, she sees 200 years of slavery, followed by 100 years of legalized segregation, harassment, and brutality. It is a bitter legacy of racism, of black people who were treated as inferior human beings.

It is only in the past 30 years that there has been a dramatic improvement in the situation for blacks. Today's black teenager might find it hard to believe that when her grandmother was young, she wasn't allowed to vote. She couldn't go into "whites-only" hotels, restaurants, and theaters unless she went in the back door as the cleaning lady. She wasn't allowed to study in white schools or worship in white churches.

Those days are gone, but unfortunately racism is still a part of American life.

Ironically, blacks and whites see the situation very differently. According to a 1990 Gallup Poll, the majority of whites in this country think blacks can get any job for which they are qualified and live in any home they can afford. Most blacks disagree.

Faye Wattleton is president of the national organization Planned Parenthood, in which she is a leading spokesperson for women's rights.

Essence, a magazine for black women, held a poll of its readers in 1989. Of the 14,000 women who responded, 83 percent agreed that racism is alive and thriving. Fewer than one percent said racism is a thing of the past.

Although affirmative action has allowed many black women to get jobs previously closed to them, it has also caused problems. Black women sometimes feel that other employees resent them as having an unfair advantage. "I am always aware by the way people relate to me that I'm black and I'm a woman," said a university administrator. "There are times you can go along with it. But there are times when you get very, very angry.

"I think there's a stigma attached to people who

come because of affirmative action," she continued. " 'You don't meet the standard because you're a minority. That's how you got in.' You're always questioned about what you do, and whether you did it right...Even the staff have been able to see the discrimination; they comment to me about it."

Many black women feel that while racism still exists, it has become less obvious.

"The new racism is more subtle, and in some ways more difficult to confront," said Karen K. Russell, daughter of former basketball star Bill Russell and a 1987 graduate of Harvard Law School.

In an article for the *New York Times Magazine* Karen discussed her experiences growing up with privilege and prejudice. She tells of coming home with her family one night and finding the house vandalized, with "NIGGA" spray-painted on the walls. Most of her father's trophies had been smashed.

In school there were thoughtless remarks and whispered slurs. She received an insulting letter that called her a "nigger bitch."

"How will I deal with racism in my life?" she asks. "On a personal level, I will ask people to explain a particular comment or joke...On the larger level, I will work with others to confront the dilemma of the widening gap between the black middle class and the black lower class, a gap that must be closed if my generation is to advance the cause of racial equality."

3 Hispanic Women

Since the United States shares a 2,000-mile-long border with Mexico, there has always been a flow of people from south to north. In the past, many Mexicans commuted between the two countries. They traveled north, usually through California or Texas, worked for a time, then returned to their homes in Mexico. Many still do this today.

Others have gone north to live. In past years, Hispanic newcomers coming from Puerto Rico and Cuba have settled in Florida, Chicago, and New York.

During the past 20 years, the flow of immigrants has turned into a flood. Along with newcomers from Mexico, Puerto Rico and Cuba have come millions of people from the Caribbean, Central America, and South America. They came to escape civil wars, political terror, and desperate economic conditions in their own countries.

As a result, the Hispanic population of the United States has grown from nine million in 1970 to more than 20 million in 1989. Some estimates predict that by the year 2025, Hispanics will surpass the black population to form the largest minority group.

Immigration is only one reason for the Hispanic population explosion. Hispanic women give birth to more children than any other group in America. In 1985, for example, 17 percent of babies born in the U.S. were Hispanic, although only seven percent of the population was Hispanic.

The Golden Cage

Millions of Hispanic women who live in the United States today are here illegally. They came into this country without the permission of the *Immigration and Naturalization Service* (INS). The INS tries to limit the number of people entering the United States each year. Unlike legal aliens, these women and their family members do not have a Resident Alien Card or *green card*, which certifies that they may live and work here.

Mexican men and women hold occupations throughout the United States, particularly in the Southwest. Some of these individuals are U.S. citizens; some are illegal aliens.

Most come from Mexico, where lack of jobs and low wages make it all but impossible to support a family. Many are laborers who are willing to do the unpleasant jobs that most U.S. citizens don't want. Since they have no passports, there is no way of knowing exactly how many illegal Hispanics are in the country. Experts estimate numbers from four million to seven million, or even as high as 12 million.

Most get in by crossing the border into Texas or California, usually at night. Many are guided by smugglers, called *coyotes*, who charge $250 to $1,000 per person for their services. If they are caught by the border guard, they spend the rest of the night in jail. The next morning they are sent back to Mexico. Most simply turn around and try again.

Thousands of women and men are brought by smugglers who supply them to employers throughout the country as cheap labor. They work in the most menial jobs—harvesting crops, sewing garments in sweatshops, washing dishes, and doing laundry. Often they are grossly underpaid and cheated by their employers. Their living conditions can be terrible. Several families might squeeze into one small apartment. Others may live in squalid shacks and boxes near the farms where they work.

Since 1985, when the Mexican government cut back expenses by laying off many of its employees, thousands of middle-class Mexicans have also joined the move north. But like the other illegal immigrants, these white-collar workers usually end up working as laborers.

Other immigrants who have come into the country illegally are from Central American countries like Guatemala and Nicaragua. Years of civil war have left their countries in ruins. Many people are starving or caught in the violent struggle between government troops and rebel soldiers. Untold numbers of men have been kidnapped, their bodies later found in a field or on a roadside. Many immigrants from these countries

The U.S. Border Patrol often raids farms to find undocumented workers who are in this country illegally. In this raid, 274 illegal aliens were found working on San Diego County, California, farms.

gamble that it is better to be homeless in the United States than to die in their own country.

Because they are here illegally, immigrants with no green card are constantly afraid of being found by *La Migra*, the INS. If they are caught, they will be deported back to their native countries.

Yet the job opportunities draw them like a magnet. Even if they work in the lowest-paying jobs, they will make much more money than they could in their native countries. And so they remain in *La Huala de Oro*—"the golden cage"— a land of wealth and opportunity where they have no legal rights or protections.

During the 1980s Congress became concerned with the flood of illegal immigrants. The result was the Immigration Reform and Control Act of 1986. For millions of Hispanics, it was a blessing and a new opportunity. For millions more, it made life more difficult.

The law offered *amnesty* from deportation to any illegal aliens who could prove they had been living in this country continuously since January 1, 1982. Farm workers who met certain qualifications also were included. They could apply for permanent resident status and eventually become citizens. For the three million immigrants who took advantage of this offer, the years of hiding from the INS were over.

But for the millions of immigrants who didn't qualify for amnesty, and who are still coming today, life in the United States has become more difficult. According to the new law, employers who hire illegal aliens may be subject to stiff fines or imprisonment. Congress had hoped this would limit the number of jobs and stop people from coming into the United States. Instead, it has just driven them deeper into the shadows.

Many immigrants were fired because they had no green cards. Jobs became much harder to find. More immigrants began working as day laborers or in low-paying underground industries. Families took their younger children out of school for fear of being found out by the INS. Older children who are citizens because they were born here dropped out of school and went to work to replace the income their parents lost.

Most experts think the tide of immigrants from Latin America will continue. As long as there is political and economic turmoil in their native countries, it will be worth the risk to enter *La Huala de Oro.*

Who Is The Hispanic Woman?

"To me it's grand. Being Hispanic gives you two beautiful cultures. It gives you your Mexican culture, which you do all possible to preserve, and your American culture, which you live daily. It's kind of like living a double life. You have two flags and two languages."

These comments from a woman in Michigan reflect the feelings of many Hispanic women in America today. They appreciate being Americans, but they also cherish the language and customs of their Latin American heritage.

This bicultural tradition has been around for many years. Hispanics, after all, began living in some parts of what is now the United States 450 years ago. Their language, customs, food and music are vital, colorful ingredients in our national culture.

Unlike other minorities in the U.S., the Hispanics are not a racial group. The term "Hispanic" refers to people who have come from Spanish-speaking countries in Central and South America, the Caribbean islands, and Mexico.

The Hispanic woman may be a member of any race: black, white, Asian, native Indian, or mixed. This is because groups of European whites, African blacks and Asians all moved to Latin America at various times in history. Many of them intermarried with the native Indians.

For many people, the word "Hispanic" means Mexican. It is true that about 63 percent of Hispanics in the United States trace their roots to Mexico, but Hispanics also come from a number of other countries. Cuba, Puerto Rico, El Salvador, Guatemala, Nicaragua, Colombia, and Ecuador are just a few.

As with any minority group, there is no "typical" Hispanic woman. She may speak only Spanish, only English, or she may be bilingual. She may be affluent or poor, well-educated or illiterate. She may be a doctor in your local hospital or a maid at a nearby hotel.

A Clash Of Cultures

About one-third of Hispanic women living in America today were born in another country. In many ways, they face the same challenges and difficulties that all immigrant women have faced. Hoping for new opportunities and a better life for themselves and their children, they have left behind family, friends, and everything that is familiar for a new country where everything is different and strange.

As with many immigrant families, there can be a clash between the culture and values of the old country and those of the new country. This is often seen in the second generation—the children of the immigrants.

Many women who come from Latin American countries are shocked by the morals and lifestyles they see here. For example, they believe American children are given too much freedom. In their own cultures, children are taught to respect authority. Strong, affectionate family bonds are valued above anything else.

Rose del Castillo Guilbault, editorial director of a San Francisco television station, said that when she was growing up, her parents clung to their Mexican traditions. Her mother often pointed out the differences between their family and *los Americanos*.

"Los Americanos talked back to their parents while we showed respect," Guilbault said. "Los Americanos were cold while we were warm and loving. Los Americanos had no morals (teenage girls went on dates without chaperones). We had morals. We didn't date."

But in school, Guilbault was faced with a different set of ideas. As a result, she grew up living in two worlds with two sets of values.

"Often, I ended up a stranger in both worlds," she said. "Reconciliation came slowly."

Hispanic Women At Work

Hispanic women hold many of the same jobs that white women do. Many are lawyers, doctors, educators and business managers. Second- and third-generation Hispanic women are getting college educations and holding professional jobs. Most Hispanic women,

Katherine Ortega held the post of U.S. Treasurer during the Reagan Administration.

however, are cashiers, typists, bookkeepers, waitresses, and child-care workers. About 60 percent of Hispanic women work at these and other low-paying jobs. As a group, Hispanic women earn about 15 percent less than white women.

As with other segments of the population, the number of Hispanic families headed by women is on the rise. Of the 4.6 million Hispanic families in the United States in 1988, one million were headed by women. More than half of those families lived below the poverty line.

Hispanic men, on the whole, also work in low-paying jobs. They earn about 33 percent less than white men. About one in four Hispanic families is below the poverty line.

One reason for the large number of impoverished

Hispanics is that so many of them are people who arrived here during the last few years. All immigrants generally start at the bottom of the economic ladder and work their way up to a more comfortable life. Studies have shown that the longer Hispanics live in the United States, the more money they make.

But Hispanics, both men and women, are not getting the education needed to help them rise out of the low-income level. Nationally, only about 60 percent of Hispanic 25-year-olds have high school diplomas. This is lower than the national average of about 76 percent and lower than any other minority group.

This problem has become worse over the past several years. In other minority groups the number of high school graduates and college students has been steadily increasing, but among Hispanics the numbers have been sliding down.

In 1984, 38 percent of Hispanic girls dropped out before finishing high school. By 1989 the number went up to 40 percent. At the same time, Hispanic women enrolling in college went from 31 percent to 30 percent.

Since most high-paying jobs require a college degree, these dropouts are committing "economic suicide," said Bill Honig, California state school superintendent. "Only 10 percent of the new jobs in the next ten years will be available to dropouts," he said.

For many Hispanic students, language has been a major stumbling block. Many come from homes where only Spanish is spoken and go to schools that do not offer bilingual education.

"I sat in a classroom for three years never understanding what was going on, and for me nothing was going on," said Gloria Molina, who later became a California assemblywoman, a Los Angeles City Council member, and the first female on the Los Angeles County Board of Supervisors.

Molina persisted in her studies, but many Hispanic students do not. Unable to break through the language barrier, they fall hopelessly behind in school.

Many of them get little help at home because their parents speak only Spanish and sometimes cannot read or write in their own language. In addition, these parents often don't encourage their children in their schoolwork because they don't appreciate the value of education. Even though an education would lead to a higher paying job later on, they make their young son or daughter work to help support the family before they finish school.

According to Guilbault, many Mexican families insist that all family members work because they dream of returning to their native village with enough money to retire or buy a business.

"Given a choice between education and work, education can take a back seat," she said. "Because in Latin American society it's not how much or what you know but whom you know and how much you have. If you leave Mexico as a poor Indian and return with an education to find work, you'll still be viewed as a poor Indian without contacts. But if you return with money, you'll be accorded more respect and, at best, control your future with your own business."

A Hispanic girl who would like to pursue an education gets little encouragement, either at home or at school. Her parents usually tell her that education is useless, or even a waste of time. Someday she will marry and her husband will take care of her. Meanwhile, it is more important for her to help support the family.

If a family can afford it, they prefer to send a boy to school. Many times an older girl is forced to drop out and get a job so she can help a brother finish his education.

A Hispanic girl with ambition may not find support at her school either. Teachers and counselors often make assumptions about her skills and goals because of her ethnic background. Rather than encouraging her to take courses that would prepare her for college, they steer her toward classes in homemaking, typing, and retailing—classes that prepare her to be a homemaker, secretary, or sales clerk.

For a Hispanic girl to succeed in school, she often has to go against what she has been taught at home. Her parents expect her to be cooperative, obedient, and respectful, while school emphasizes independence and competition.

Hispanic females are supposed to submit to the will of the men in their lives: fathers, brothers, and husbands. A young woman who does well in school and goes on to college is not staying in her traditional place. She feels torn between her obligations to her family and her own ambitions.

Living Without A Green Card

Hispanic women who are here illegally and don't work tend to stay in their homes, out of sight. They leave only to buy groceries or go to church. Most don't get welfare or other public assistance because they think they might be traced by *La Migra*. Many are afraid to seek medical attention when they are sick, or prenatal care when they are pregnant.

Women without a green card who work usually end up in difficult, low-paying jobs as laborers, housekeepers, or agricultural workers. Frequently they are cheated by employers who pay them less than the legal minimum wage, and there's nothing they can do about it. Sometimes employers even promise payment for a certain amount of work and then refuse to pay when the work is done. The women don't complain to the authorities because they are afraid of being deported.

"I feel trapped, but I can't change jobs because they'll ask me for a work permit, and I don't have one," said a Mexican woman who earns about $80 a week at a Los Angeles garment manufacturing shop. "It's depressing to work all day for so little, but there's not much I can do about it."

Gloria Estefan, a popular singer and songwriter, comes from a Hispanic background. Here, she holds the American Music Award she won in 1989.

Families without legal work permits are often split up. Fathers and sons slip across the border to work. They regularly send money back to their families in Mexico and occasionally go back for a visit. Sometimes women also commute back and forth between a divided family.

One woman left her six youngest children with her mother in Guadalajara to join her three older children and her husband in East Los Angeles. Traveling between the two exhausted her strength and her savings.

"My heart is broken every time I leave for Mexico, and it's broken every time I come back," she said. "I see no solution to my problem."

4 Asian-American Women

Suddenly they were here. Millions of Asians moving to America. They came from Vietnam, Cambodia, Laos, Korea, China, India, and the Philippines.

These people wasted no time settling in. They moved their large families into homes and apartments, then got jobs or set up businesses. Some even became millionaires.

Their children went to school and studied hard, often performing better than the other students. They started wearing American clothes, eating American food, and learning the American lifestyle. Many finished college and entered high-paying professions.

The accomplishment of the Asians who poured into this country during the past two decades has been so impressive that they have been called "the model minority," an example of what education, discipline, and hard work can do.

It's true that many Asians have found success in this country, but for many it hasn't been that easy. And some haven't thrived at all.

Success And Disappointment

Of course, not all people of Asian descent in America are newcomers. Many are the descendents of Japanese, Chinese, and Filipino immigrants who came to America more than 100 years ago.

Most of the women in these families have become thoroughly Americanized. Those who are employed work in the same jobs as white women, often earning above-average salaries.

In the past 20 years there has been an explosive growth in the Asian-American population, from one-and-one-half million in 1970 to nearly seven million today. Nearly three million of them are newcomers to our country.

The immigrants from China, the Philippines, Korea, and India came here hoping to find political freedom,

Recent immigrants to this country, like these Hmong women from Laos, often experience discrimination.

good jobs, and a better life. Most of them did find jobs. Those who brought along their savings often used the money to buy a store, motel, or other small business. Americans saw them as very successful.

But the immigrants themselves are often disappointed and frustrated. Many were architects, engineers, and doctors in their own countries, but they are unable to practice their craft here. Instead, they work long hours running their own businesses. Others work in factories, restaurants, or other low-paying jobs. Women who were educated to become teachers, scientists, doctors, and nurses end up working as office clerks, hospital orderlies, or store keepers.

Many immigrants who don't speak English find that language is a major barrier. Some have to deal with employers who are prejudiced against Asians. Others discover that degrees and licenses earned in their own countries do not qualify them to practice their profession in the United States.

One veterinarian came from the Philippines, hoping to continue her practice here. But first she found that she would have to pass an English test, complete a one-year internship at a veterinary hospital without pay, and pass an examination to qualify for her license. While she was fulfilling those requirements, she supported her family by working as a clerk in an insurance company. After seven years she obtained her license.

In New York and San Francisco, where many Chinese immigrants have settled, the women often end up working as seamstresses in garment factories. They work long hours, six days a week, and are paid by the piece. Their pay is very low, but they don't complain about the wages and working conditions. They are afraid that if they lose their jobs they won't be able to find another.

"If you know just a little English, you can go to an office and get a job cleaning up," said one Chinese woman. "It has more security, more benefits. But how are you going to get a job like that if you don't know a little English? And how are you going to learn English if you have to work 12 hours a day, six days a week and then come home and take care of your family?"

Refugees

Like most of the people who have moved to America over the years, immigrants from China, Korea, the Philippines, and India were eager to come. They planned their trip and prepared for their arrival in America as best they could.

But the people who have come from Southeast Asia

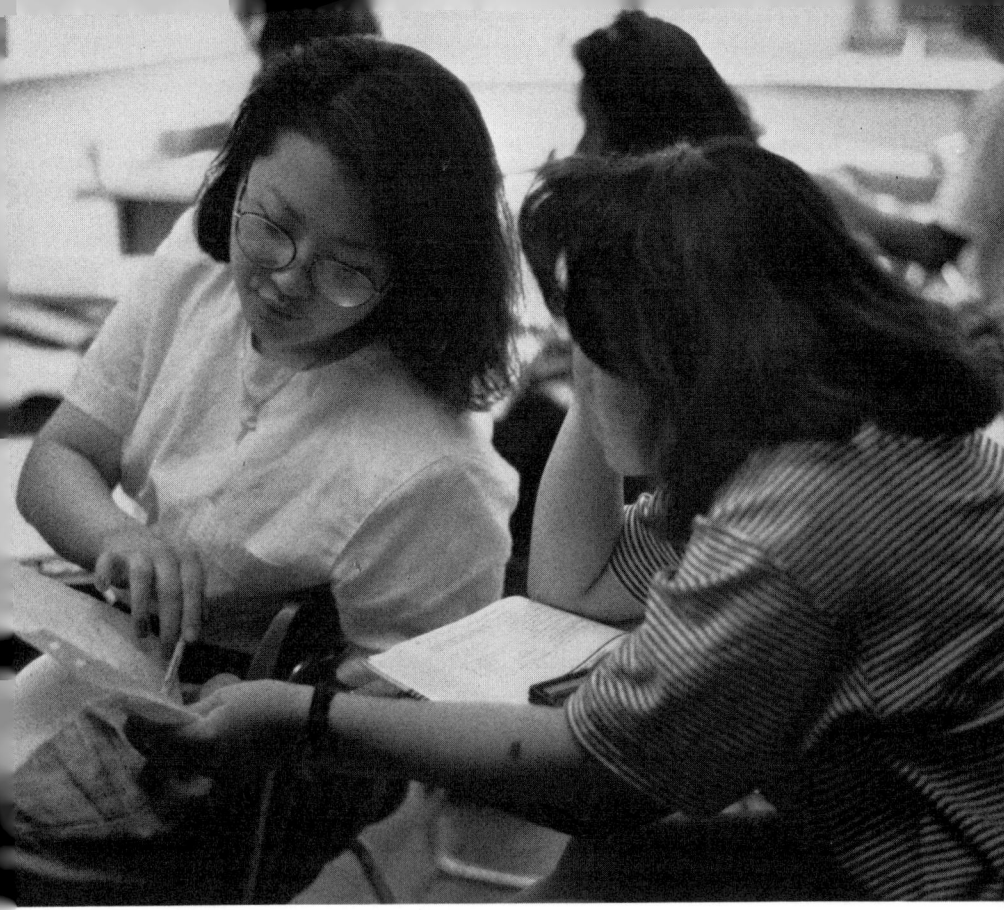

Many young Asian refugees who have grown up in the U. S. have worked hard to earn excellent grades in school. Because of this, Asian students as a group have been stereotyped as academically aggressive students.

during the past two decades have been *refugees*, not immigrants. Their countries—Vietnam, Laos, and Cambodia—were torn apart by 30 years of war. The dictators who took over those countries hunted down people who did not support them or who helped Americans during the Vietnam War. These people knew that if they stayed in their own countries, there was a good chance they would starve, end up in a prison or work camp, or be killed. So they escaped to America.

The first wave of refugees left with the Americans at the end of the war in 1975. The evacuation of the American troops and their Vietnamese supporters was a time of great panic and confusion. Many people left on a moment's notice, bringing only what they could carry. Some had only the clothes they were wearing.

The refugees in this first group were primarily well-educated, wealthy professionals. Most of them spoke English. Many had studied abroad and had friends in the United States who helped them get established. Some managed to bring their savings with them. For them, getting settled in the United States was relatively easy. Many prospered within a short time.

Things weren't so easy for the second wave who escaped from Southeast Asia during the next several years. Their trips were dangerous, traumatic ordeals, and thousands died along the way. Many were women whose husbands had been killed or imprisoned. Alone, they guided their children to safety. By some estimates, one in ten died trying to leave their country. Those who survived often spent months in refugee camps before being sent to their new homes in Canada, Europe, Australia, or America.

For these refugees—the *boat people*—settling in America was much more difficult than it had been for the first group. Those in the second group, for the most part, were uneducated farming people. They spoke little English and had few skills that they could use to get jobs here. They worked in the lowest-paying occupations. Often they had two jobs, which left little time to learn English or new skills that might help them get better jobs. As a result, many of the boat people still live in poverty.

Emotional Scars

Many of the women who endured these events have lasting emotional scars. They are depressed and anxious, and they have trouble sleeping. They can't forget what they have seen: family members killed before their eyes, children starving in their arms. Some were separated from their children during the war or while they were escaping and have been unable to find them again.

"I wish someone could hear me scream and cry, 'Where are my children? Where are my children?'" said one Cambodian woman.

"I don't know what happiness is anymore," said another. Four of her eleven children died before she could leave her country. "I still don't know whether I can ever be happy again. It is too hard to think of hope."

Along with their sorrows, the women from Southeast Asia must deal with the shock of adjusting to a new country. Everything seems strange and uncomfortable to them. In their own countries they lived in familiar, closely-knit communities. Family and friends were always nearby to provide help and comfort when it was needed. Here, the families are scattered. Younger family members are gone at school or at work. Older women often end up alone and isolated in their homes.

"The main problem that I have in America is that I don't know how to speak English," said an elderly Vietnamese woman. "Second, if I wanted to go somewhere, I cannot. I would have to use a car, but I cannot drive. If I use the bus, I am afraid that I will become lost."

A Clash Of Cultures

Most of the younger refugee women have found jobs and learned how to get around in their new country. But they are still homesick and lonely for family members who were left behind. Many hope they will be able to go back to their country of birth someday. America is still a strange country to them, with lifestyles and values they don't understand. It's not surprising that many of them cling fiercely to their old traditions and beliefs, at least in their own homes.

This presents problems for their teenage daughters, who either came here as young children or were born here. Since they grew up in the United States, this

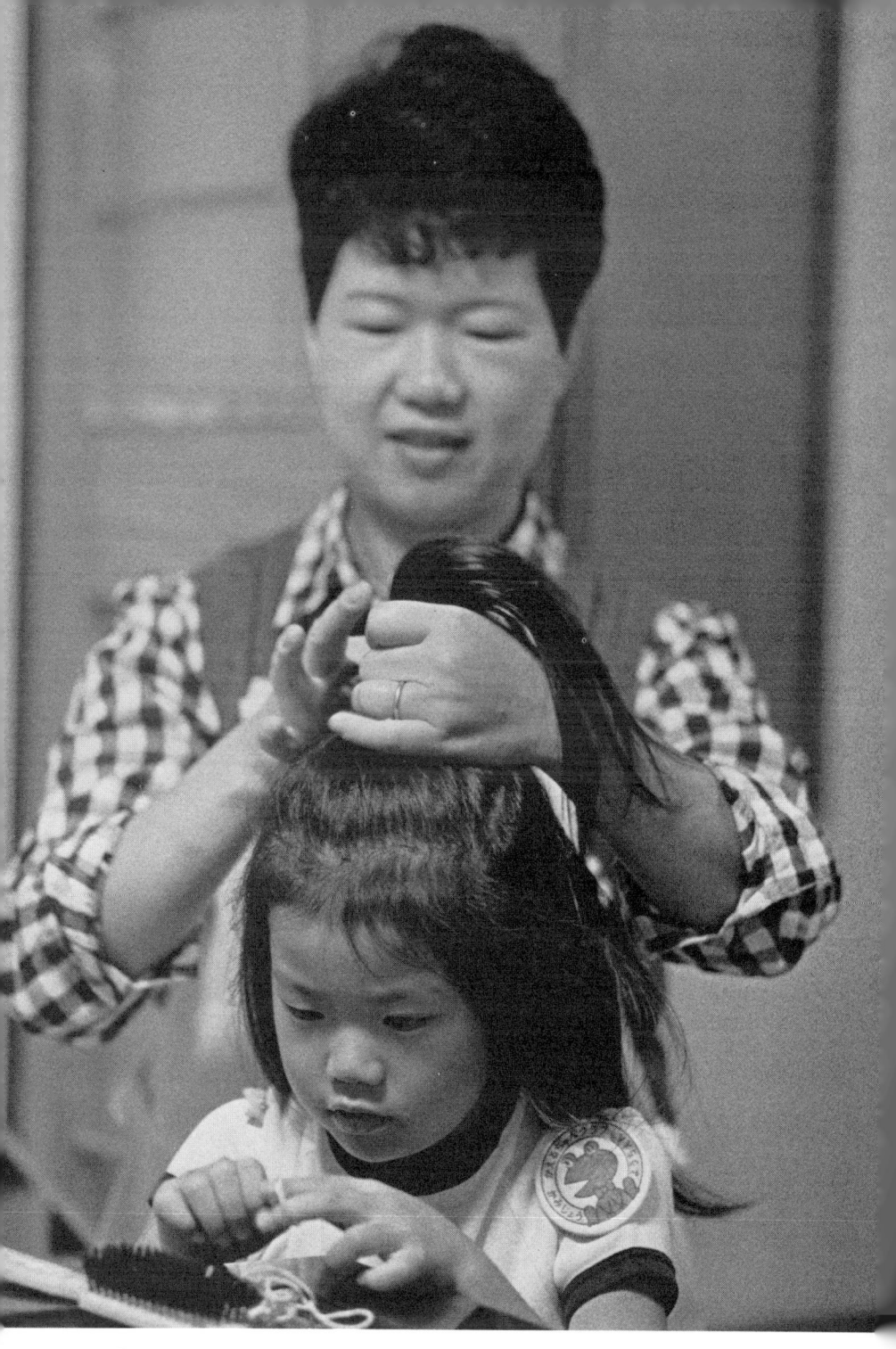
The family is an especially strong force in the lives of Asian Americans.

Asian-American Connie Chung is a respected anchorperson for NBC News.

country is not strange to them, as it is for their parents. The teenagers speak fluent English, participate in school activities, and often work part-time. In most ways, they are typical American girls. But when they get home, they enter a different world. Here they must respect the ancient customs and rules of the old country.

An Asian-American girl is expected to be quiet and obedient, and to serve her father. She may not date, drive a car, or go to a party unless a brother also attends. Her parents expect to choose a husband for her.

"The rules are different at home than at school," said a 16-year-old Cambodian-American girl. "We respect our father and mother as gods. I could never find the heart to disobey them."

Many Asian customs are based on the teachings of the ancient Chinese philosopher Confucius. He taught that women should be *subservient* (obedient) to men and that the needs of the group must come before the needs of the individual. These ideas are a part of life in Asia, but they clash with ideals in America.

For Asian-American girls, the conflict is particularly difficult because their parents want them to be proper, obedient women. At the same time, they also expect them to get a good education and good jobs. So these young women find themselves pulled between two worlds.

Some can't handle the strain caused by this conflict. Psychologists and social workers who serve the Asian-American community say many young girls have trouble adjusting to their dual lives. Some run away from home, turn to drugs or prostitution, or attempt suicide. But most manage to reconcile their two worlds or find ways of compromising with their parents.

"For a while I challenged them, but it's pretty much instilled in me now," said a 19-year-old Korean-American girl. "I'm like a combination of Korean and American, right in the middle."

5 *A Look At The '80s*

Many women of color believe that the 1980s were a disastrous time for minorities in America. Because of changes in the economy and government policy, the lower economic classes grew larger and slid deeper into poverty. These classes included large portions of the minority population, particularly single mothers.

During the 1960s and 1970s, the federal government had taken an active role in helping the poor and promoting the rights and economic advancement of women and minorities. That began to change, however, when Ronald Reagan became President in 1980. Many people who voted for him believed that government was spending too much on social programs. Many said that the programs failed to do what they promised.

Poor people, it was said, had become too dependent on government and lost the will and initiative to climb America's ladder of opportunity. In other words, the poor should help themselves.

Reducing taxes was a high priority for President Reagan. He convinced Congress to save money by drastically cutting funds for social programs such as housing assistance, anti-poverty projects, and health services for the poor. Programs that provided job training and helped people find employment were practically eliminated.

Cuts in these programs had a drastic impact on millions of minority women, particularly single mothers, who lived below the poverty line.

On the other hand, the Reagan years were a time of prosperity for many. Reagan believed that a healthy economy would benefit everyone, like "a rising tide lifts all boats." For many this was true.

"This country is really booming," said a black tobacco farmer in Maryland. "Making a decent living is the first thing. And race is the second thing."

Other blacks said that Reagan's policies brought

black people closer together and inspired a new sense of self-reliance.

Equal Opportunity And Affirmative Action

In the help-wanted section of the newspaper, many companies include "EOE" in their advertisements for employees. This stands for "Equal Opportunity Employer." It means that the company will not discriminate against anyone in their hiring practices.

Thirty years ago, companies would never say this. In fact, many refused to hire women or members of minority groups. Women and minorities who were hired usually stayed in the lowest ranks of a company, even if they were qualified for better positions.

During the 1960s, the civil rights movement and the feminist movement demanded changes that led to equal opportunity and affirmative action programs. These plans were designed to correct the injustices of the past by assuring women and minorities that they would be hired, promoted, and treated fairly by employers.

The Equal Employment Opportunity Commission (EEOC) was created by the Civil Rights Act of 1964. It is a permanent organization that tries to eliminate hiring and job promotion practices that discriminate against people because of their race, color, religion, sex, or national origin. The commission investigates complaints by employees and may take legal action against companies that violate laws against discrimination.

A presidential executive order in 1965 was the first to call for affirmative action programs. Rather than just being able to prove they weren't discriminating, companies doing business with the federal government had to provide plans and timetables by which they would increase the number of women and minorities they hired. Affirmative action programs were also established in colleges and universities to help women and minorities get an education that would qualify

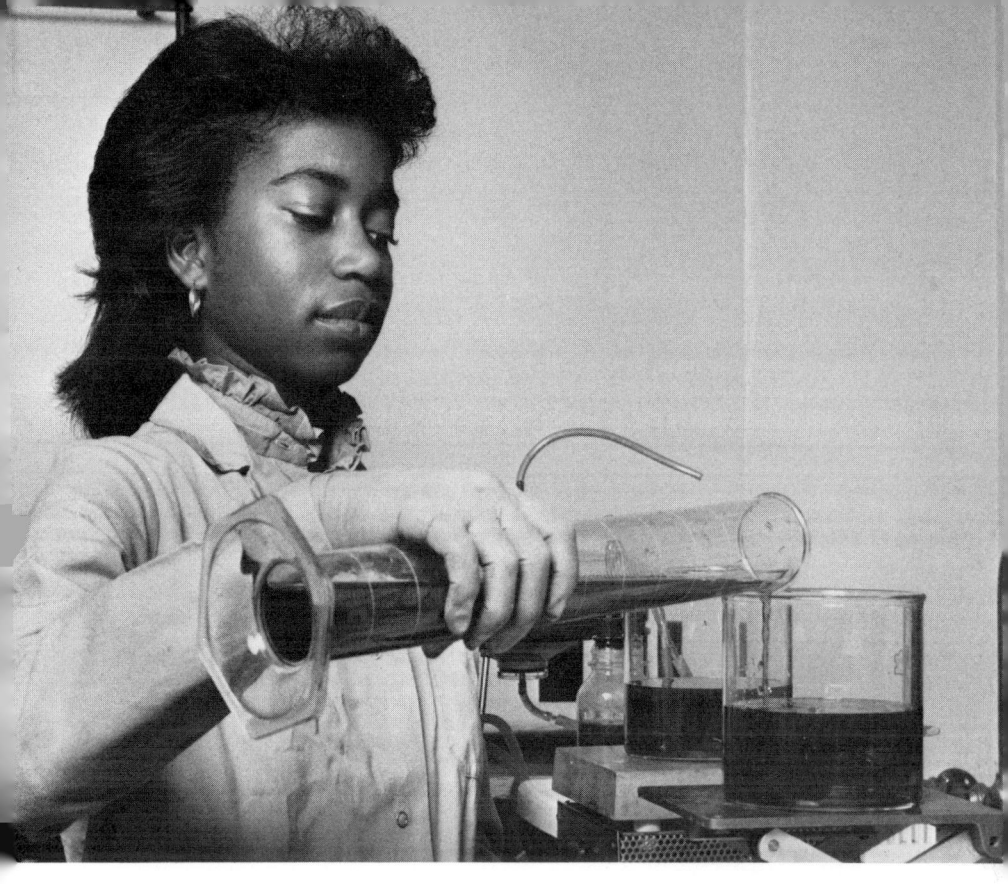

Minority women are slowly gaining opportunity and education to enter fields once dominated by white males, such as scientific research.

them for better jobs.

Many experts believe these programs played a vital part in improving the employment opportunities and financial standing of minorities.

"Affirmative action is the most important modern antidiscrimination technique ever instituted in the United States," said Eleanor Holmes Norton, a black professor at Georgetown University Law Center and former head of the EEOC. "It is the one tool that has had a demonstrable effect on discrimination....In just one decade—the 1970s—the number of sales, technical and professional jobs blacks held increased by 50 percent. Affirmative action, by all statistical measures, has been the central ingredient to the creation of the black middle class."

Some experts, on the other hand, believe that

49

affirmative action has outlived its usefulness. One of them is Glenn C. Loury, a black professor of political economy at Harvard University's John F. Kennedy School of Government. He contends that racism in the workplace is much less common now than it was 20 years ago.

"So now, even though the nature of discrimination has lessened, there is still a reliance on affirmative action," he said. "It has become something of a crutch. Set-asides [positions reserved for women or minorities], for example, should be temporary, to get business started, not entitlements people expect. This is unfair both to other people and to the people it should benefit."

Many white males resent affirmative action programs, calling them a form of "reverse discrimination." They protest that they are losing jobs to less-qualified workers who were hired or promoted only because of their race or gender. Companies complain that they are bogged down in EEOC paperwork and that they are afraid to fire incompetent employees who happen to be women or minorities.

In 1978, Allan Bakke, a white student, sued the medical school at the University of California at Davis after he failed to get in. The school had reserved 16 out of 100 available slots for people of color. Bakke complained that this was unfair because some of the minorities who were admitted were less qualified (based on test scores) than some of the white males who were not. He took his case to the Supreme Court and won.

When Ronald Reagan became president in 1980, he immediately declared his opposition to affirmative action programs. During his term of office, he appointed three conservative justices to the Supreme Court. This tipped the overall balance of the court toward his conservative way of thinking.

As a direct result of Reagan's nominations, the

Although affirmative action has made a difference, most minority women, like most all women in the United States, still work in fields that are stereotyped as "women's work," like teaching or clerical jobs.

Supreme Court later made a number of decisions that further weakened affirmative action programs. It became more difficult for women and minorities to win discrimination cases. For example, the court ruled that an employee who wanted to sue a company for unfair treatment would have to prove that the company deliberately practiced discrimination. Previously, it had been up to the company to prove that it lacked minority or women employees because of other business requirements.

President George Bush has taken a firm stand in opposition to hiring quotas. In October 1990, he vetoed the Civil Rights Act of 1990, which had been passed by overwhelming majorities in both houses of Congress. The bill would have banned racial harassment on the

Many minority women are earning respect as superior amateur and professional athletes, such as figure skating champion Debbie Thomas. After the 1988 Olympics, Debbie returned to Stanford University, where she was a pre-med student.

job and made it easier for women and minorities to win discrimination cases. Bush said that the bill would have forced companies to adopt hiring quotas as a way of avoiding lawsuits, even though it specifically stated that nothing in it "shall be construed to require or encourage quotas."

In November 1990, Senator Jesse Helms of North Carolina was reelected to the Senate. Observers give a great deal of credit for his successful campaign to one of his television commercials. It showed the hands of a white person crumpling up a letter of rejection from an employer. The narrator said: "You needed that job, but they had to give it to a minority because of a racial quota. Is that really fair?"

The controversy over affirmative action is likely to continue. Eventually, however, the argument may become irrelevant. Within 20 years, most people entering the labor force will be minorities and women.

6 Into The Future

Until recently the United States has been a country populated by a large majority of white people and small groups of blacks, Hispanics and Asians.

That will change during the next several decades. If immigration and birth rates continue at their current rates, the Hispanic and Asian segments of the population will increase by about 40 percent, while the black population will grow by about 15 percent. The number of whites, meanwhile, will grow by only three percent. By the year 2050, whites will be in the minority.

In some parts of the country the changes are already quite obvious. California, for instance, is the state having the most ethnic and racial diversity. Minorities account for 42 percent of the population.

While it may sound like America will be bursting at the seams if immigrants keep pouring in, this is not really the case. Most American families are having fewer children than they did in the past. Some researchers say that if immigrants stopped coming, the population of the United States would actually start dropping within 50 years. According to one study, the country will need 464,000 immigrants every year for the next 100 years in order to keep the population in 2100 the same size as it was in 1980.

Needless to say, these changes will have a major impact on women of color. As their numbers increase, and as more of them become second- and third-generation Americans, their influence in the workplace and in politics is bound to increase. By the year 2050, they may have enough clout to solve the problems they deal with now. Perhaps by then, racism and sexism will be just memories of the past.

The New Workplace

By the year 2000, American corporations that insist on having white males as their top executives will have to search long and hard. By that time, according to current estimates, only nine percent of people entering the work force will be white, non-Hispanic, and male.

Thirty percent of the new labor force will be black, Hispanic, and Asian women. Combined with white women, who will represent another 28 percent, women of all colors will be the moving force in tomorrow's pool of employees.

A number of progressive companies have already responded to this change. They have brought more women and minorities into management positions and found ways to accommodate the special needs of their women employees.

One example is Pitney Bowes, a large office equipment company based in Connecticut. Since 1985 this company has had a 35-15 plan. At least 35 percent of all new employees must be women, and at least 15 percent must be members of a minority. Ten years ago there were almost no female top executives in the company. Today, 17 percent of the corporate officers are women. US West, a telephone company in Denver, Colorado, established a Women of Color Accelerated Development Program to train black and Hispanic women employees for management positions.

More companies are also making an effort to help working mothers balance their responsibilities at home and at work. These companies are making it easier for women to get flexible schedules or reduced work hours if they need more time for their children. Women can pass up a possible promotion to meet other family needs if they so desire without losing their future chances for advancement. And some companies offer in-house day-care.

Corporate executives are aware of school drop-out rates among some minority groups. They are concerned that before long they won't be able to find enough employees who have the high-level skills required for jobs of the future. Some company officials have decided to act.

In 1988, for example, Tenneco Inc. "adopted" Jefferson Davis High School, an inner-city school with mostly Hispanic students in Houston, Texas. The company donated money to the school and provided tutors. As a result, the number of students who passed the state's basic proficiency test jumped from 19 percent to 55 percent.

Young Hispanic mothers in Houston have benefited from a program called *Avance* (the Spanish word for "advance"). Sponsored by General Foods Corp., the program teaches parenting skills to poor mothers who have small children. After attending the program, one young woman left her abusive husband, finished her high school education, and went on to get a college degree.

"Hispanics haven't been brought up to value education," she said. "I realized at Avance, it was only me who could offer my children something."

Politics

Until recently, women of color had little political power. They had no money and no organizations to promote their causes. Many of those who were eligible to vote did not go to the polls, so their voices weren't heard. They were ignored by the people in political office.

These women were even ignored, to a large extent, by the political movements of the '60s. In the groups organized to win civil rights for black people and Hispanics, they were expected to support their men. If they became involved in feminist groups, they were accused of breaking ranks in the fight for racial equality.

The feminist movement, on the other hand, was largely organized by white, middle-class women. They were the ones who benefited the most from it. Most women of color felt that their needs (such as better education and health care) were overlooked by the feminist movement.

Sharon Pratt Dixon became the first woman mayor of Washington, D.C., in 1990.

All that is changing. Women of color are beginning to reach for political power on their own. At the local level, they are starting to have success. They are winning seats on school boards, city councils, and state legislatures. One black woman, Cardiss Collins of Illinois, and one Hispanic, Ileana Ros-Lehtinen of Florida, have been elected to Congress.

Minority women have started political action committees and organizations to support women candidates. One such organization is *Comision Femenil Mexicana Nacional*, which is based in Los Angeles.

"The reason Latinas want to run for political office is to make issues very important to them and their community a priority," said Maggie Cervantes, president of the group. "A number of these women have their eye on higher office and within this decade, you'll see them elected."

As the numbers of minority women grow, more of them will become well-educated, and politically active. They will vote in greater numbers, and many more will be elected to political office. Undoubtedly their needs and concerns will no longer be ignored.

Into The Next Century

One way or another, the road to the next century is bound to be bumpy for everybody. The population of America will be going through enormous changes, and many people don't like change. Some people still think that only white people are "real" Americans. They resent Asians and Hispanics. Often immigrants inspire anger no matter what they do. If they are successful, they are envied and accused of taking away jobs from other Americans. If they are poor, they are seen as a burden on society. If they are illegal, they are seen as a national menace.

There will continue to be competition for political power and jobs between men and women, between whites and minorities, and even among the minority groups themselves. There will be anger, perhaps violence. But there also will be intermarriages, compromises, and new solutions.

America has always been a land of immigrants and diversity. Many historians believe that it is the constant flow of immigrants, with their different ideas and cultures, that keeps America vital and successful. And although racism and discrimination persist, the hundreds of ethnic groups and races in America, by and large, live together in peace. Few countries in the world can say that.

Glossary

AFFIRMATIVE ACTION. Policies that use plans and timetables to increase the number of women and minorities who are employed and promoted by businesses and accepted to colleges and universities.

AMNESTY. A pardon offered by a government that removes the penalties for criminal or political offenses. In the case of illegal immigrants, some received amnesty for violations of immigration regulations.

CIVIL RIGHTS MOVEMENT. The social revolution that occurred from the mid-1950s through 1960s to give black Americans the same opportunities as white Americans.

COYOTE. A smuggler who helps illegal immigrants cross the border from Mexico into the United States.

FEMINISM. The belief that women should have the same rights and opportunities as men.

FEMINIZATION OF POVERTY. When large numbers of single mothers fell below the poverty line in the past two decades. Many are minorities.

GREEN CARD. A resident alien card issued by the Immigration and Naturalization Service that proves an immigrant is legally entitled to live and work in the United States.

IMMIGRATION AND NATURALIZATION SERVICE (INS). An office of the United States government that regulates who is qualified to enter as an immigrant. The INS tries to control the number of people coming into the country. It also regulates the process by which immigrants become citizens.

LA MIGRA. The Hispanic term for the INS.

PINK COLLAR JOBS. Jobs that traditionally have been held by women.

POVERTY LINE. A measurement used by the government to determine how many people live in poverty in this country. In 1988, a family of four that had an average yearly income of $12,092 or less was considered below the poverty line.

RACISM. The belief that one's own race is superior to others.

REFUGEE. A person forced to emigrate from their native land by political or environmental problems.

SEGREGATION. The separation of people by race in schools, housing, businesses and other public places.

SEXISM. The belief that males are superior to females.

WHITE COLLAR JOBS. Professions that do not require manual labor. These jobs generally are located in offices and usually require formal clothing, such as suits.

Bibliography

Books

Blauner, Bob. *Black Lives, White Lives.* Berkeley: University of California Press, 1989.

Freeman, James A. *Hearts of Sorrow: Vietnamese-American Lives.* Stanford, CA: Stanford University Press, 1989.

Mirande, Alfredo and Evangelina Enriquez. *La Chicana.* Chicago: The University of Chicago Press, 1979.

Takaki, Ronald. *Strangers from a Different Shore.* Boston: Little, Brown and Company, 1989.

U.S. Department of Labor, Women's Bureau. *20 Facts on Women Workers.* Washington, D.C.: U.S. Government Printing Office, 1990.

Women in Management. Washington, D.C.: U.S. Government Printing Office, 1989.

Women of Hispanic Origin in the Labor Force. Washington, D.C.: U.S. Printing Office, 1989.

Wright, John W., ed. *The Universal Almanac, 1991.* Kansas City: Andrews and McNeel, 1990.

Periodicals

Castro, Janice. "Get Set: Here They Come!" *Time,* Fall, 1990 Special Issue: 50-52.

Eng, Lily. "Treating the Torment." *Los Angeles Times,* January 4, 1990: E1.

Garcia, Dawn. "Latinas Opening Political Doors." *San Francisco Chronicle,* October 18, 1990: A1.

Guilbault, Rose del Castillo. "The American Dream has its Price." *San Francisco Chronicle,* March 5, 1989: 3.

"One Foot Here, One Foot Back Home." *San Francisco Chronicle,* June 24, 1990: 5.

Haldane, David. "Asian Girls: A Cultural Tug of War." *Los Angeles Times,* September 24, 1988: I1.

Harrison, Bennett. "For Blacks, a Degree Doesn't Always Automatically Mean Higher Incomes." *Los Angeles Times,* September 2, 1990: M,4.

Helmore, Kristin. "Middle-class Mexicans go North." *Christian Science Monitor,* February 25, 1988: 1.

Henry, William A. "Beyond the Melting Pot." *Time,* April 9, 1990: 28-31.

"Here's What You Think." *Essence,* June, 1989: 70.

Hernandez, Marita. "Millions Bypassed by Amnesty Fear Future." *Los Angeles Times,* April 3, 1988: I1.

Ladner, Joyce A. "Our Families—Then and Now." *Essence,* May, 1990: 180-182.

Mason, Todd. "Can Business Throw a Net Under Hispanic Dropouts" *Business Week,* February 20, 1989): 151-154.

May, Lee. "Blacks Look Back in Anger at Reagan Years." *Los Angeles Times,* January 20, 1989: I,1.

Randolph, Laura B. "What Can We Do about the Most Explosive Problem in Black America: The Widening Gap between Women who are Making it and Men who Aren't." *Ebony,* August 1990): 52-56.

Russell, Karen K. "Growing Up with Privilege and Prejudice." *New York Times Magazine,* June 14, 1987: 23-28.

Sands, Josefina. "Black Women at Work." *Essence,* May, 1990: 58-60.

Villarosa, Linda. "What Have They Done for Us Lately?" *Essence,* May, 1990: 66-70.

"Voices of Hispanic America." *Hispanic,* December 1990): 26.

Wallis, Claudia. "Onward, Women!" *Time,* December 4, 1989:80-89.

Picture Credits

AP Wide World Photos: 7, 14, 17, 18, 20, 24, 26, 30, 34, 44, 52, 54, 58
The Image Works: 12 (Bob Daemmrich); 22 (Alan Carey); 40;
    49 (Harriet Gans)
Photo Researchers, Inc.,: 4, 46 (Chester Higgins Jr.); 10 (Spencer Grant); 36 (Renee Lynn); 38 (Katrina Thomas); 43 (Robert Isaacs); 51 (Kathy Sloane)

Index

affirmative action, 13, 20-21, 48-53
African-American women *see* black women
Asian-American women
  and birth rate, 55
  and culture clash, 42-45
  and language barrier, 39, 42
  earnings, 6
  emotional scars, 41-42
  occupations, 38-39
  origins, 37, 39-41
  population growth, 37
  reasons for emigration, 37-38
black women
  and birth rate, 55
  and education, 11, 13
  and racism, 19-21
  and shortage of black men, 15-16
  and unemployment, 8
  as head of households, 13
  below the poverty line, 13-15
  earnings, 6, 11, 13
  in public office, 12
  rate of teenage pregnancy, 16-17
  success compared with black men, 12-13
boat people, 41 *see also* refugees
civil rights movement, 6, 11, 48, 57
Equal Employment Opportunity Commission (EEOC), 48-50 *see also* affirmative action
feminist movement, 6, 11, 48, 57
feminization of poverty, 7
Hispanic-American women
  and bicultural tradition, 27-28
  and birth rate, 23, 55
  and clash of values, 28-29, 32-33
  and education, 30-33, 57
  and language barrier, 31
  and unemployment, 8
  at work, 29, 33-35
  below the poverty line, 29
  definition of Hispanic, 28
  earnings, 6, 29, 35
  in politics, 58-59
  origins, 23, 27-28
  reasons for emigration, 23, 25
immigrant women
  adjusting to America, 9
  as laborers, 25
  earnings, 6, 30
  illegals, 23-27
  reasons for emigration, 25
minority women
  and federal spending, 47-48
  and rate of immigration, 55
  below the poverty line, 8
  earnings, 13
  in management, 7, 56
  joining the labor force, 53-57
pink collar occupations, 6
poverty line, 7-8
racism, 8-9, 19-21, 50 *see also* black women
refugees, 39-41
single mothers, 7-8, 17, 47
women
  as portrayed on television, 5, 11
  in management, 6-7, 56
  on crack, 19
  working mothers, 8